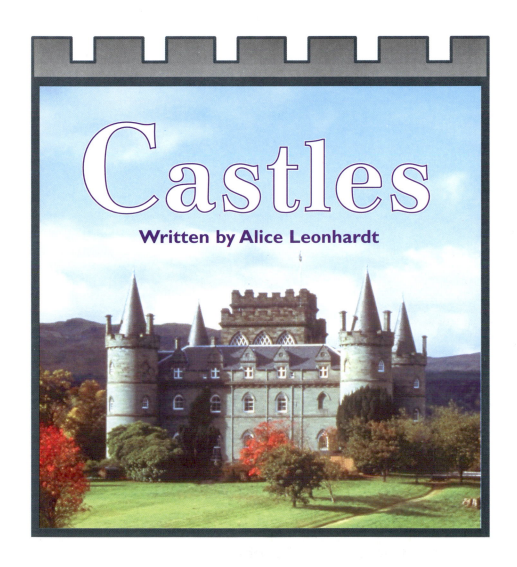

Castles

Written by Alice Leonhardt

STECK-VAUGHN
ELEMENTARY · SECONDARY · ADULT · LIBRARY

A Harcourt Classroom Education Company

www.steck-vaughn.com

This pile of stones stands on a hill in Scotland.

Once there were many stones.

Once many people lived here.

Long ago these stones were part of a castle.

Most castles were built hundreds of years ago.

Many kings and queens had castles built.

They wanted to protect their people.

They wanted to protect their land, too.

Many castles were built on low ground.

People living in them could come and go easily.

Some castles were built on hills or by rivers.

An enemy had a hard time getting to these castles.

The first castles were made of wood and dirt.

They were easy for an enemy to burn.

Later castles were made of stone.

Building with stone took many, many workers.

Castle walls were very tall.

A tall wall was hard for an enemy to climb.

Castle walls were thick, too.

People could walk on top of the thick walls.

Some castle walls had towers along them.

People often lived in the towers.

Some castles had moats around them.

A moat was a deep ditch filled with water.

A castle with a moat also had a drawbridge.

The drawbridge was a bridge over the moat.

People could raise the drawbridge.

Then an enemy couldn't get over the moat.

Inside the castle walls lay a big courtyard.

Hay and firewood were stored there.

People worked in the courtyard, too.

They made tools and chopped wood.

The people of a castle needed a lot of food.

Many castles had gardens.

In the gardens people grew plants to eat.

People also grew pretty plants to look at.

Most castles had a large room called a great hall.

Feasts were held in the great hall.

These large meals went on for hours.

People ate geese, eels, pies, and puddings.

The kitchen of a castle was a busy place.

Cooks worked at big tables to make foods.

They baked bread in a stone oven.

They cooked meat over an open fire.

A king and his family often had their own tower.

Their tower often stood at the center of the castle.

It had bedrooms and a living room.

But it did not have closets.

Open fires heated the family's living room.

The family sat in chairs made of wood.

Some living rooms were very fancy.

They had beautiful paintings and ceilings.

People still live in some castles.

Windsor Castle, in England, is the home of a queen.

Windsor Castle has 15 towers.

It was built more than 600 years ago.

Today many castles are museums.

Visitors climb towers and explore rooms.

They dream about kings and queens.

They dream about living in a castle long ago.